# MAKING MEMORIES
# ONE CAMPING
# AT A TIME!

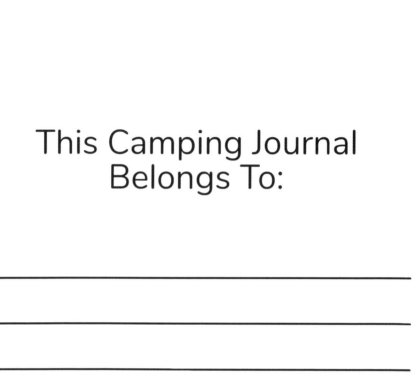

# This Camping Journal Belongs To:

_____

_____

_____

# Notes

| # | Campground | Location | Rating |
|---|---|---|---|
| 1 | | | ☆ ☆ ☆ ☆ ☆ |
| 2 | | | ☆ ☆ ☆ ☆ ☆ |
| 3 | | | ☆ ☆ ☆ ☆ ☆ |
| 4 | | | ☆ ☆ ☆ ☆ ☆ |
| 5 | | | ☆ ☆ ☆ ☆ ☆ |
| 6 | | | ☆ ☆ ☆ ☆ ☆ |
| 7 | | | ☆ ☆ ☆ ☆ ☆ |
| 8 | | | ☆ ☆ ☆ ☆ ☆ |
| 9 | | | ☆ ☆ ☆ ☆ ☆ |
| 10 | | | ☆ ☆ ☆ ☆ ☆ |
| 11 | | | ☆ ☆ ☆ ☆ ☆ |
| 12 | | | ☆ ☆ ☆ ☆ ☆ |
| 13 | | | ☆ ☆ ☆ ☆ ☆ |
| 14 | | | ☆ ☆ ☆ ☆ ☆ |
| 15 | | | ☆ ☆ ☆ ☆ ☆ |
| 16 | | | ☆ ☆ ☆ ☆ ☆ |
| 17 | | | ☆ ☆ ☆ ☆ ☆ |
| 18 | | | ☆ ☆ ☆ ☆ ☆ |
| 19 | | | ☆ ☆ ☆ ☆ ☆ |
| 20 | | | ☆ ☆ ☆ ☆ ☆ |
| 21 | | | ☆ ☆ ☆ ☆ ☆ |
| 22 | | | ☆ ☆ ☆ ☆ ☆ |
| 23 | | | ☆ ☆ ☆ ☆ ☆ |
| 24 | | | ☆ ☆ ☆ ☆ ☆ |
| 25 | | | ☆ ☆ ☆ ☆ ☆ |

| # | Campground | Location | Rating |
|---|---|---|---|
| 26 | | | ☆ ☆ ☆ ☆ ☆ |
| 27 | | | ☆ ☆ ☆ ☆ ☆ |
| 28 | | | ☆ ☆ ☆ ☆ ☆ |
| 29 | | | ☆ ☆ ☆ ☆ ☆ |
| 30 | | | ☆ ☆ ☆ ☆ ☆ |
| 31 | | | ☆ ☆ ☆ ☆ ☆ |
| 32 | | | ☆ ☆ ☆ ☆ ☆ |
| 33 | | | ☆ ☆ ☆ ☆ ☆ |
| 34 | | | ☆ ☆ ☆ ☆ ☆ |
| 35 | | | ☆ ☆ ☆ ☆ ☆ |
| 36 | | | ☆ ☆ ☆ ☆ ☆ |
| 37 | | | ☆ ☆ ☆ ☆ ☆ |
| 38 | | | ☆ ☆ ☆ ☆ ☆ |
| 39 | | | ☆ ☆ ☆ ☆ ☆ |
| 40 | | | ☆ ☆ ☆ ☆ ☆ |
| 41 | | | ☆ ☆ ☆ ☆ ☆ |
| 42 | | | ☆ ☆ ☆ ☆ ☆ |
| 43 | | | ☆ ☆ ☆ ☆ ☆ |
| 44 | | | ☆ ☆ ☆ ☆ ☆ |
| 45 | | | ☆ ☆ ☆ ☆ ☆ |
| 46 | | | ☆ ☆ ☆ ☆ ☆ |
| 47 | | | ☆ ☆ ☆ ☆ ☆ |
| 48 | | | ☆ ☆ ☆ ☆ ☆ |
| 49 | | | ☆ ☆ ☆ ☆ ☆ |
| 50 | | | ☆ ☆ ☆ ☆ ☆ |

Campground:_____

Location:_____

Site #:____ Ideal Site #:____ Date:_____

| Check In:        Check Out: | Location | ☆ ☆ ☆ ☆ ☆ |
|---|---|---|
| Weather: ☀ ⛅ ☁ 🌧 ⛈ | Amenities | ☆ ☆ ☆ ☆ ☆ |
| WIFI: Good ☐ Bad ☐ None ☐ | Cleanliness | ☆ ☆ ☆ ☆ ☆ |
| Pad Type: Dirt ☐ Concrete ☐ | Activities | ☆ ☆ ☆ ☆ ☆ |
| Total Cost Per Night: | Security | ☆ ☆ ☆ ☆ ☆ |

## Notes

Overall Rating: ☆ ☆ ☆ ☆ ☆       1

We went camping with: _____

_____

The new people and friends that we met: _____

_____

Our favorite thing to do at this campground was: _____

_____

Favorite food (recipes, shops, restaurants, etc.): _____

_____

We visited these cool places: _____

_____

Our favorite activities that we did were: _____

_____

Things we want to do and see next time: _____

_____

Memorable moments or memories: _____

_____

_____

Campground: _____

Location: _____

Site #: _____ Ideal Site #: _____ Date: _____

| Check In:          Check Out: | Location | ☆ ☆ ☆ ☆ ☆ |
|---|---|---|
| Weather: ☀ ⛅ ☁ 🌧 ⛈ | Amenities | ☆ ☆ ☆ ☆ ☆ |
| WIFI: Good ☐ Bad ☐ None ☐ | Cleanliness | ☆ ☆ ☆ ☆ ☆ |
| Pad Type: Dirt ☐ Concrete ☐ | Activities | ☆ ☆ ☆ ☆ ☆ |
| Total Cost Per Night: | Security | ☆ ☆ ☆ ☆ ☆ |

## Notes

Overall Rating: ☆ ☆ ☆ ☆ ☆     2

We went camping with: _____

_____

_____

The new people and friends that we met: _____

_____

_____

Our favorite thing to do at this campground was: _____

_____

_____

Favorite food (recipes, shops, restaurants, etc.): _____

_____

_____

We visited these cool places: _____

_____

_____

Our favorite activities that we did were: _____

_____

_____

Things we want to do and see next time: _____

_____

_____

Memorable moments or memories: _____

_____

_____

Campground:

Location:

Site #:_____ Ideal Site #:_____ Date:_____

| Check In:        Check Out: | Location | ☆ ☆ ☆ ☆ ☆ |
|---|---|---|
| Weather: ☀ ⛅ ☁ 🌧 ⛈ | Amenities | ☆ ☆ ☆ ☆ ☆ |
| WIFI: Good ☐ Bad ☐ None ☐ | Cleanliness | ☆ ☆ ☆ ☆ ☆ |
| Pad Type: Dirt ☐ Concrete ☐ | Activities | ☆ ☆ ☆ ☆ ☆ |
| Total Cost Per Night: | Security | ☆ ☆ ☆ ☆ ☆ |

## Notes

Overall Rating: ☆ ☆ ☆ ☆ ☆

We went camping with:

The new people and friends that we met:

Our favorite thing to do at this campground was:

Favorite food (recipes, shops, restaurants, etc.):

We visited these cool places:

Our favorite activities that we did were:

Things we want to do and see next time:

Memorable moments or memories:

Campground: _____

Location: _____

Site #: _____ Ideal Site #: _____ Date: _____

| Check In: | Check Out: | Location | ☆ ☆ ☆ ☆ ☆ |
| Weather: ☀ 🌤 ☁ 🌧 ⛈ | | Amenities | ☆ ☆ ☆ ☆ ☆ |
| WIFI: Good ☐ Bad ☐ None ☐ | | Cleanliness | ☆ ☆ ☆ ☆ ☆ |
| Pad Type: Dirt ☐ Concrete ☐ | | Activities | ☆ ☆ ☆ ☆ ☆ |
| Total Cost Per Night: | | Security | ☆ ☆ ☆ ☆ ☆ |

## Notes

Overall Rating: ☆ ☆ ☆ ☆ ☆

We went camping with:_____

_____

The new people and friends that we met:_____

_____

Our favorite thing to do at this campground was:_____

_____

Favorite food (recipes, shops, restaurants, etc.):_____

_____

We visited these cool places:_____

_____

Our favorite activities that we did were:_____

_____

Things we want to do and see next time:_____

_____

Memorable moments or memories:_____

_____

_____

_____

Campground: _____

Location: _____

Site #: _____ Ideal Site #: _____ Date: _____

| Check In:      Check Out: | Location | ☆ ☆ ☆ ☆ ☆ |
| --- | --- | --- |
| Weather: ☀ ⛅ ☁ 🌧 ⛈ | Amenities | ☆ ☆ ☆ ☆ ☆ |
| WIFI: Good ☐ Bad ☐ None ☐ | Cleanliness | ☆ ☆ ☆ ☆ ☆ |
| Pad Type: Dirt ☐ Concrete ☐ | Activities | ☆ ☆ ☆ ☆ ☆ |
| Total Cost Per Night: | Security | ☆ ☆ ☆ ☆ ☆ |

## Notes

Overall Rating: ☆ ☆ ☆ ☆ ☆     5

We went camping with:_____

_____

The new people and friends that we met:_____

_____

Our favorite thing to do at this campground was:_____

_____

Favorite food (recipes, shops, restaurants, etc.):_____

_____

We visited these cool places:_____

_____

Our favorite activities that we did were:_____

_____

Things we want to do and see next time:_____

_____

Memorable moments or memories:_____

_____

_____

Campground: _____

Location: _____

Site #: _____ Ideal Site #: _____ Date: _____

| Check In:     Check Out: | Location | ☆ ☆ ☆ ☆ ☆ |
|---|---|---|
| Weather: ☼ ⛅ ☁ 🌧 ⛈ | Amenities | ☆ ☆ ☆ ☆ ☆ |
| WIFI: Good ☐ Bad ☐ None ☐ | Cleanliness | ☆ ☆ ☆ ☆ ☆ |
| Pad Type: Dirt ☐ Concrete ☐ | Activities | ☆ ☆ ☆ ☆ ☆ |
| Total Cost Per Night: | Security | ☆ ☆ ☆ ☆ ☆ |

## Notes

Overall Rating: ☆ ☆ ☆ ☆ ☆

We went camping with:_____

_____

The new people and friends that we met:_____

_____

Our favorite thing to do at this campground was:_____

_____

Favorite food (recipes, shops, restaurants, etc.):_____

_____

We visited these cool places:_____

_____

Our favorite activities that we did were:_____

_____

Things we want to do and see next time:_____

_____

Memorable moments or memories:_____

_____

_____

Campground:_____

Location:_____

Site #:_____ Ideal Site #:_____ Date:_____

| Check In:        Check Out: | Location | ☆ ☆ ☆ ☆ ☆ |
| --- | --- | --- |
| Weather: ☀ ⛅ ☁ 🌧 ⛈ | Amenities | ☆ ☆ ☆ ☆ ☆ |
| WIFI: Good ☐ Bad ☐ None ☐ | Cleanliness | ☆ ☆ ☆ ☆ ☆ |
| Pad Type: Dirt ☐ Concrete ☐ | Activities | ☆ ☆ ☆ ☆ ☆ |
| Total Cost Per Night: | Security | ☆ ☆ ☆ ☆ ☆ |

## Notes

Overall Rating: ☆ ☆ ☆ ☆ ☆    7

We went camping with:_____

_____

_____

The new people and friends that we met:_____

_____

_____

Our favorite thing to do at this campground was:_____

_____

_____

Favorite food (recipes, shops, restaurants, etc.):_____

_____

_____

We visited these cool places:_____

_____

_____

Our favorite activities that we did were:_____

_____

_____

Things we want to do and see next time:_____

_____

_____

Memorable moments or memories:_____

_____

_____

_____

Campground: _____

Location: _____

Site #: _____ Ideal Site #: _____ Date: _____

| Check In: | Check Out: | Location | ☆ ☆ ☆ ☆ ☆ |
|---|---|---|---|
| Weather: ☀ ⛅ ☁ 🌧 ⛈ | | Amenities | ☆ ☆ ☆ ☆ ☆ |
| WIFI: Good ☐ Bad ☐ None ☐ | | Cleanliness | ☆ ☆ ☆ ☆ ☆ |
| Pad Type: Dirt ☐ Concrete ☐ | | Activities | ☆ ☆ ☆ ☆ ☆ |
| Total Cost Per Night: | | Security | ☆ ☆ ☆ ☆ ☆ |

## Notes

Overall Rating: ☆ ☆ ☆ ☆ ☆

We went camping with:

_____

The new people and friends that we met:

_____

Our favorite thing to do at this campground was:

_____

Favorite food (recipes, shops, restaurants, etc.):

_____

We visited these cool places:

_____

Our favorite activities that we did were:

_____

Things we want to do and see next time:

_____

Memorable moments or memories:

_____

Campground:_____

Location:_____

Site #:_____ Ideal Site #:_____ Date:_____

| Check In:     Check Out: | Location | ☆ ☆ ☆ ☆ ☆ |
|---|---|---|
| Weather: ☼ ⛅ ☁ 🌧 ⛈ | Amenities | ☆ ☆ ☆ ☆ ☆ |
| WIFI: Good ☐ Bad ☐ None ☐ | Cleanliness | ☆ ☆ ☆ ☆ ☆ |
| Pad Type: Dirt ☐ Concrete ☐ | Activities | ☆ ☆ ☆ ☆ ☆ |
| Total Cost Per Night: | Security | ☆ ☆ ☆ ☆ ☆ |

## Notes

Overall Rating: ☆ ☆ ☆ ☆ ☆    9

We went camping with:_____

_____

_____

The new people and friends that we met:_____

_____

_____

Our favorite thing to do at this campground was:_____

_____

_____

Favorite food (recipes, shops, restaurants, etc.):_____

_____

_____

We visited these cool places:_____

_____

_____

Our favorite activities that we did were:_____

_____

_____

Things we want to do and see next time:_____

_____

_____

Memorable moments or memories:_____

_____

_____

Campground:_____

Location:_____

Site #:_____ Ideal Site #:_____ Date:_____

| Check In: | Check Out: | Location | ☆ ☆ ☆ ☆ ☆ |
|---|---|---|---|
| Weather: ☀ ⛅ ☁ 🌧 ⛈ | | Amenities | ☆ ☆ ☆ ☆ ☆ |
| WIFI: Good ☐ Bad ☐ None ☐ | | Cleanliness | ☆ ☆ ☆ ☆ ☆ |
| Pad Type: Dirt ☐ Concrete ☐ | | Activities | ☆ ☆ ☆ ☆ ☆ |
| Total Cost Per Night: | | Security | ☆ ☆ ☆ ☆ ☆ |

## Notes

Overall Rating: ☆ ☆ ☆ ☆ ☆    10

We went camping with: _____

_____

_____

The new people and friends that we met: _____

_____

_____

Our favorite thing to do at this campground was: _____

_____

_____

Favorite food (recipes, shops, restaurants, etc.): _____

_____

_____

We visited these cool places: _____

_____

_____

Our favorite activities that we did were: _____

_____

_____

Things we want to do and see next time: _____

_____

_____

Memorable moments or memories: _____

_____

_____

_____

Campground:_____

Location:_____

Site #:_____ Ideal Site #:_____ Date:_____

| Check In:          Check Out: | Location | ☆ ☆ ☆ ☆ ☆ |
| --- | --- | --- |
| Weather: ☀ ⛅ ☁ 🌧 ⛈ | Amenities | ☆ ☆ ☆ ☆ ☆ |
| WIFI: Good ☐ Bad ☐ None ☐ | Cleanliness | ☆ ☆ ☆ ☆ ☆ |
| Pad Type: Dirt ☐ Concrete ☐ | Activities | ☆ ☆ ☆ ☆ ☆ |
| Total Cost Per Night: | Security | ☆ ☆ ☆ ☆ ☆ |

## Notes

Overall Rating: ☆ ☆ ☆ ☆ ☆     11

We went camping with: _____

_____

_____

The new people and friends that we met: _____

_____

_____

Our favorite thing to do at this campground was: _____

_____

_____

Favorite food (recipes, shops, restaurants, etc.): _____

_____

_____

We visited these cool places: _____

_____

_____

Our favorite activities that we did were: _____

_____

_____

Things we want to do and see next time: _____

_____

_____

Memorable moments or memories: _____

_____

_____

Campground:_____

Location:_____

Site #:_____ Ideal Site #:_____ Date:_____

| Check In:        Check Out: | Location | ☆ ☆ ☆ ☆ ☆ |
|---|---|---|
| Weather: ☀ ⛅ ☁ 🌧 ⛈ | Amenities | ☆ ☆ ☆ ☆ ☆ |
| WIFI: Good ☐ Bad ☐ None ☐ | Cleanliness | ☆ ☆ ☆ ☆ ☆ |
| Pad Type: Dirt ☐ Concrete ☐ | Activities | ☆ ☆ ☆ ☆ ☆ |
| Total Cost Per Night: | Security | ☆ ☆ ☆ ☆ ☆ |

## Notes

Overall Rating: ☆ ☆ ☆ ☆ ☆

We went camping with:_____

_____

_____

The new people and friends that we met:_____

_____

_____

Our favorite thing to do at this campground was:_____

_____

_____

Favorite food (recipes, shops, restaurants, etc.):_____

_____

_____

We visited these cool places:_____

_____

_____

Our favorite activities that we did were:_____

_____

_____

Things we want to do and see next time:_____

_____

_____

Memorable moments or memories:_____

_____

_____

Campground:_____

Location:_____

Site #:_____ Ideal Site #:_____ Date:_____

| Check In:        Check Out: | Location | ☆ ☆ ☆ ☆ ☆ |
|---|---|---|
| Weather: ☀ ⛅ ☁ 🌧 ⛈ | Amenities | ☆ ☆ ☆ ☆ ☆ |
| WIFI: Good ☐ Bad ☐ None ☐ | Cleanliness | ☆ ☆ ☆ ☆ ☆ |
| Pad Type: Dirt ☐ Concrete ☐ | Activities | ☆ ☆ ☆ ☆ ☆ |
| Total Cost Per Night: | Security | ☆ ☆ ☆ ☆ ☆ |

## Notes

Overall Rating: ☆ ☆ ☆ ☆ ☆        13

We went camping with: _____

_____

The new people and friends that we met: _____

_____

Our favorite thing to do at this campground was: _____

_____

Favorite food (recipes, shops, restaurants, etc.): _____

_____

We visited these cool places: _____

_____

Our favorite activities that we did were: _____

_____

Things we want to do and see next time: _____

_____

Memorable moments or memories: _____

_____

_____

Campground: _____

Location: _____

Site #: _____ Ideal Site #: _____ Date: _____

| | | Location | ☆ ☆ ☆ ☆ ☆ |
|---|---|---|---|
| Check In: Check Out: | | Location | ☆ ☆ ☆ ☆ ☆ |
| Weather: ☀ ⛅ ☁ 🌧 ⛈ | | Amenities | ☆ ☆ ☆ ☆ ☆ |
| WIFI: Good ☐ Bad ☐ None ☐ | | Cleanliness | ☆ ☆ ☆ ☆ ☆ |
| Pad Type: Dirt ☐ Concrete ☐ | | Activities | ☆ ☆ ☆ ☆ ☆ |
| Total Cost Per Night: | | Security | ☆ ☆ ☆ ☆ ☆ |

## Notes

Overall Rating: ☆ ☆ ☆ ☆ ☆          14

We went camping with:_____

_____

The new people and friends that we met:_____

_____

Our favorite thing to do at this campground was:_____

_____

Favorite food (recipes, shops, restaurants, etc.):_____

_____

We visited these cool places:_____

_____

Our favorite activities that we did were:_____

_____

Things we want to do and see next time:_____

_____

Memorable moments or memories:_____

_____

_____

Campground: _____

Location: _____

Site #: _____ Ideal Site #: _____ Date: _____

| Check In: _____ Check Out: _____ | Location | ☆ ☆ ☆ ☆ ☆ |
| Weather: ☼ ⛅ ☁ 🌧 ⛈ | Amenities | ☆ ☆ ☆ ☆ ☆ |
| WIFI: Good ☐ Bad ☐ None ☐ | Cleanliness | ☆ ☆ ☆ ☆ ☆ |
| Pad Type: Dirt ☐ Concrete ☐ | Activities | ☆ ☆ ☆ ☆ ☆ |
| Total Cost Per Night: | Security | ☆ ☆ ☆ ☆ ☆ |

## Notes

Overall Rating: ☆ ☆ ☆ ☆ ☆  15

We went camping with:_____

_____

_____

The new people and friends that we met:_____

_____

_____

Our favorite thing to do at this campground was:_____

_____

_____

Favorite food (recipes, shops, restaurants, etc.):_____

_____

_____

We visited these cool places:_____

_____

_____

Our favorite activities that we did were:_____

_____

_____

Things we want to do and see next time:_____

_____

_____

Memorable moments or memories:_____

_____

_____

Campground:_____

Location:_____

Site #:_____ Ideal Site #:_____ Date:_____

| Check In:        Check Out: | Location | ☆ ☆ ☆ ☆ ☆ |
| --- | --- | --- |
| Weather: ☀ ⛅ ☁ 🌧 ⛈ | Amenities | ☆ ☆ ☆ ☆ ☆ |
| WIFI: Good ☐ Bad ☐ None ☐ | Cleanliness | ☆ ☆ ☆ ☆ ☆ |
| Pad Type: Dirt ☐ Concrete ☐ | Activities | ☆ ☆ ☆ ☆ ☆ |
| Total Cost Per Night: | Security | ☆ ☆ ☆ ☆ ☆ |

## Notes

Overall Rating: ☆ ☆ ☆ ☆ ☆

We went camping with: _____

_____

The new people and friends that we met: _____

_____

Our favorite thing to do at this campground was: _____

_____

Favorite food (recipes, shops, restaurants, etc.): _____

_____

We visited these cool places: _____

_____

Our favorite activities that we did were: _____

_____

Things we want to do and see next time: _____

_____

Memorable moments or memories: _____

_____

_____

Campground:_____

Location:_____

Site #:_____ Ideal Site #:_____ Date:_____

| Check In:         Check Out: | Location | ☆ ☆ ☆ ☆ ☆ |
|---|---|---|
| Weather: ☀ ⛅ ☁ 🌧 ⛈ | Amenities | ☆ ☆ ☆ ☆ ☆ |
| WIFI: Good ☐ Bad ☐ None ☐ | Cleanliness | ☆ ☆ ☆ ☆ ☆ |
| Pad Type: Dirt ☐ Concrete ☐ | Activities | ☆ ☆ ☆ ☆ ☆ |
| Total Cost Per Night: | Security | ☆ ☆ ☆ ☆ ☆ |

## Notes

Overall Rating: ☆ ☆ ☆ ☆ ☆      17

We went camping with: _____

The new people and friends that we met: _____

Our favorite thing to do at this campground was: _____

Favorite food (recipes, shops, restaurants, etc.): _____

We visited these cool places: _____

Our favorite activities that we did were: _____

Things we want to do and see next time: _____

Memorable moments or memories: _____

Campground: _____

Location: _____

Site #: ____ Ideal Site #: ____ Date: _____

| | | |
|---|---|---|
| Check In: ____ Check Out: ____ | Location | ☆ ☆ ☆ ☆ ☆ |
| Weather: ☀ ⛅ ☁ 🌧 ⛈ | Amenities | ☆ ☆ ☆ ☆ ☆ |
| WIFI: Good ☐ Bad ☐ None ☐ | Cleanliness | ☆ ☆ ☆ ☆ ☆ |
| Pad Type: Dirt ☐ Concrete ☐ | Activities | ☆ ☆ ☆ ☆ ☆ |
| Total Cost Per Night: | Security | ☆ ☆ ☆ ☆ ☆ |

## Notes

Overall Rating: ☆ ☆ ☆ ☆ ☆   18

We went camping with:_____

The new people and friends that we met:_____

Our favorite thing to do at this campground was:_____

Favorite food (recipes, shops, restaurants, etc.):_____

We visited these cool places:_____

Our favorite activities that we did were:_____

Things we want to do and see next time:_____

Memorable moments or memories:_____

Campground:_____

Location:_____

Site #:_____ Ideal Site #:_____ Date:_____

| Check In:        Check Out: | Location | ☆ ☆ ☆ ☆ ☆ |
|---|---|---|
| Weather: ☀ ⛅ ☁ 🌧 ⛈ | Amenities | ☆ ☆ ☆ ☆ ☆ |
| WIFI: Good ☐ Bad ☐ None ☐ | Cleanliness | ☆ ☆ ☆ ☆ ☆ |
| Pad Type: Dirt ☐ Concrete ☐ | Activities | ☆ ☆ ☆ ☆ ☆ |
| Total Cost Per Night: | Security | ☆ ☆ ☆ ☆ ☆ |

## Notes

Overall Rating: ☆ ☆ ☆ ☆ ☆          19

We went camping with: _____

_____

The new people and friends that we met: _____

_____

Our favorite thing to do at this campground was: _____

_____

Favorite food (recipes, shops, restaurants, etc.): _____

_____

We visited these cool places: _____

_____

Our favorite activities that we did were: _____

_____

Things we want to do and see next time: _____

_____

Memorable moments or memories: _____

_____

_____

Campground:_____

Location:_____

Site #:_____ Ideal Site #:_____ Date:_____

| Check In:          Check Out: | Location | ☆ ☆ ☆ ☆ ☆ |
|---|---|---|
| Weather: ☀ ⛅ ☁ 🌧 ⛈ | Amenities | ☆ ☆ ☆ ☆ ☆ |
| WIFI: Good ☐ Bad ☐ None ☐ | Cleanliness | ☆ ☆ ☆ ☆ ☆ |
| Pad Type: Dirt ☐ Concrete ☐ | Activities | ☆ ☆ ☆ ☆ ☆ |
| Total Cost Per Night: | Security | ☆ ☆ ☆ ☆ ☆ |

## Notes

Overall Rating: ☆ ☆ ☆ ☆ ☆    20

We went camping with: _____

_____

_____

The new people and friends that we met: _____

_____

_____

Our favorite thing to do at this campground was: _____

_____

_____

Favorite food (recipes, shops, restaurants, etc.): _____

_____

_____

We visited these cool places: _____

_____

_____

Our favorite activities that we did were: _____

_____

_____

Things we want to do and see next time: _____

_____

_____

Memorable moments or memories: _____

_____

_____

Campground:_____

Location:_____

Site #:_____ Ideal Site #:_____ Date:_____

| Check In:       Check Out: | Location | ☆ ☆ ☆ ☆ ☆ |
| Weather: ☀ ⛅ ☁ 🌧 ⛈ | Amenities | ☆ ☆ ☆ ☆ ☆ |
| WIFI: Good ☐ Bad ☐ None ☐ | Cleanliness | ☆ ☆ ☆ ☆ ☆ |
| Pad Type: Dirt ☐ Concrete ☐ | Activities | ☆ ☆ ☆ ☆ ☆ |
| Total Cost Per Night: | Security | ☆ ☆ ☆ ☆ ☆ |

## Notes

Overall Rating: ☆ ☆ ☆ ☆ ☆   21

We went camping with:_____

_____

The new people and friends that we met:_____

_____

Our favorite thing to do at this campground was:_____

_____

Favorite food (recipes, shops, restaurants, etc.):_____

_____

We visited these cool places:_____

_____

Our favorite activities that we did were:_____

_____

Things we want to do and see next time:_____

_____

Memorable moments or memories:_____

_____

_____

Campground:_____

Location:_____

Site #:_____ Ideal Site #:_____ Date:_____

| Check In:          Check Out: | Location | ☆ ☆ ☆ ☆ ☆ |
| Weather: ☀ ⛅ ☁ 🌧 ⛈ | Amenities | ☆ ☆ ☆ ☆ ☆ |
| WIFI: Good ☐ Bad ☐ None ☐ | Cleanliness | ☆ ☆ ☆ ☆ ☆ |
| Pad Type: Dirt ☐ Concrete ☐ | Activities | ☆ ☆ ☆ ☆ ☆ |
| Total Cost Per Night: | Security | ☆ ☆ ☆ ☆ ☆ |

## Notes

Overall Rating: ☆ ☆ ☆ ☆ ☆   22

We went camping with: _____

_____

_____

The new people and friends that we met: _____

_____

_____

Our favorite thing to do at this campground was: _____

_____

_____

Favorite food (recipes, shops, restaurants, etc.): _____

_____

_____

We visited these cool places: _____

_____

_____

Our favorite activities that we did were: _____

_____

_____

Things we want to do and see next time: _____

_____

_____

Memorable moments or memories: _____

_____

_____

Campground:_____

Location:_____

Site #:_____ Ideal Site #:_____ Date:_____

| Check In:        Check Out: | Location | ☆ ☆ ☆ ☆ ☆ |
| Weather: ☀ ⛅ ☁ 🌧 ⛈ | Amenities | ☆ ☆ ☆ ☆ ☆ |
| WIFI: Good ☐ Bad ☐ None ☐ | Cleanliness | ☆ ☆ ☆ ☆ ☆ |
| Pad Type: Dirt ☐ Concrete ☐ | Activities | ☆ ☆ ☆ ☆ ☆ |
| Total Cost Per Night: | Security | ☆ ☆ ☆ ☆ ☆ |

## Notes

Overall Rating: ☆ ☆ ☆ ☆ ☆   23

We went camping with: _____

_____

The new people and friends that we met: _____

_____

Our favorite thing to do at this campground was: _____

_____

Favorite food (recipes, shops, restaurants, etc.): _____

_____

We visited these cool places: _____

_____

Our favorite activities that we did were: _____

_____

Things we want to do and see next time: _____

_____

Memorable moments or memories: _____

_____

_____

Campground:_____

Location:_____

Site #:_____ Ideal Site #:_____ Date:_____

| Check In:        Check Out: | Location | ☆ ☆ ☆ ☆ ☆ |
| Weather: ☀ ⛅ ☁ 🌧 ⛈ | Amenities | ☆ ☆ ☆ ☆ ☆ |
| WIFI: Good ☐ Bad ☐ None ☐ | Cleanliness | ☆ ☆ ☆ ☆ ☆ |
| Pad Type: Dirt ☐ Concrete ☐ | Activities | ☆ ☆ ☆ ☆ ☆ |
| Total Cost Per Night: | Security | ☆ ☆ ☆ ☆ ☆ |

## Notes

Overall Rating: ☆ ☆ ☆ ☆ ☆

We went camping with:_____

_____

The new people and friends that we met:_____

_____

Our favorite thing to do at this campground was:_____

_____

Favorite food (recipes, shops, restaurants, etc.):_____

_____

We visited these cool places:_____

_____

Our favorite activities that we did were:_____

_____

Things we want to do and see next time:_____

_____

Memorable moments or memories:_____

_____

_____

Campground:_____

Location:_____

Site #:_____ Ideal Site #:_____ Date:_____

| Check In:         Check Out: | Location | ☆ ☆ ☆ ☆ ☆ |
|---|---|---|
| Weather: ☀ ⛅ ☁ 🌧 ⛈ | Amenities | ☆ ☆ ☆ ☆ ☆ |
| WIFI: Good ☐ Bad ☐ None ☐ | Cleanliness | ☆ ☆ ☆ ☆ ☆ |
| Pad Type: Dirt ☐ Concrete ☐ | Activities | ☆ ☆ ☆ ☆ ☆ |
| Total Cost Per Night: | Security | ☆ ☆ ☆ ☆ ☆ |

## Notes

Overall Rating: ☆ ☆ ☆ ☆ ☆        25

We went camping with:_____

_____

The new people and friends that we met:_____

_____

Our favorite thing to do at this campground was:_____

_____

Favorite food (recipes, shops, restaurants, etc.):_____

_____

We visited these cool places:_____

_____

Our favorite activities that we did were:_____

_____

Things we want to do and see next time:_____

_____

Memorable moments or memories:_____

_____

_____

Campground:_____

Location:_____

Site #:_____ Ideal Site #:_____ Date:_____

| Check In: Check Out: | Location | ☆ ☆ ☆ ☆ ☆ |
|---|---|---|
| Weather: ☀ ⛅ ☁ 🌧 ⛈ | Amenities | ☆ ☆ ☆ ☆ ☆ |
| WIFI: Good ☐ Bad ☐ None ☐ | Cleanliness | ☆ ☆ ☆ ☆ ☆ |
| Pad Type: Dirt ☐ Concrete ☐ | Activities | ☆ ☆ ☆ ☆ ☆ |
| Total Cost Per Night: | Security | ☆ ☆ ☆ ☆ ☆ |

## Notes

Overall Rating: ☆ ☆ ☆ ☆ ☆    26

We went camping with: _____

_____

_____

The new people and friends that we met: _____

_____

_____

Our favorite thing to do at this campground was: _____

_____

_____

Favorite food (recipes, shops, restaurants, etc.): _____

_____

_____

We visited these cool places: _____

_____

_____

Our favorite activities that we did were: _____

_____

_____

Things we want to do and see next time: _____

_____

_____

Memorable moments or memories: _____

_____

_____

Campground:_____

Location:_____

Site #:_____ Ideal Site #:_____ Date:_____

| Check In: | Check Out: | Location | ☆ ☆ ☆ ☆ ☆ |
|---|---|---|---|
| Weather: ☀ ⛅ ☁ 🌧 ⛈ | | Amenities | ☆ ☆ ☆ ☆ ☆ |
| WIFI: Good ☐ Bad ☐ None ☐ | | Cleanliness | ☆ ☆ ☆ ☆ ☆ |
| Pad Type: Dirt ☐ Concrete ☐ | | Activities | ☆ ☆ ☆ ☆ ☆ |
| Total Cost Per Night: | | Security | ☆ ☆ ☆ ☆ ☆ |

## Notes

Overall Rating: ☆ ☆ ☆ ☆ ☆    27

We went camping with:_____

_____

_____

The new people and friends that we met:_____

_____

_____

Our favorite thing to do at this campground was:_____

_____

_____

Favorite food (recipes, shops, restaurants, etc.):_____

_____

_____

We visited these cool places:_____

_____

_____

Our favorite activities that we did were:_____

_____

_____

Things we want to do and see next time:_____

_____

_____

Memorable moments or memories:_____

_____

_____

Campground:_____

Location:_____

Site #:_____ Ideal Site #:_____ Date:_____

| Check In:        Check Out: | Location | ☆ ☆ ☆ ☆ ☆ |
|---|---|---|
| Weather: ☀ ⛅ ☁ 🌧 ⛈ | Amenities | ☆ ☆ ☆ ☆ ☆ |
| WIFI: Good ☐ Bad ☐ None ☐ | Cleanliness | ☆ ☆ ☆ ☆ ☆ |
| Pad Type: Dirt ☐ Concrete ☐ | Activities | ☆ ☆ ☆ ☆ ☆ |
| Total Cost Per Night: | Security | ☆ ☆ ☆ ☆ ☆ |

## Notes

Overall Rating: ☆ ☆ ☆ ☆ ☆     28

We went camping with:_____
_____

The new people and friends that we met:_____
_____

Our favorite thing to do at this campground was:_____
_____

Favorite food (recipes, shops, restaurants, etc.):_____
_____

We visited these cool places:_____
_____

Our favorite activities that we did were:_____
_____

Things we want to do and see next time:_____
_____

Memorable moments or memories:_____
_____
_____
_____

Campground:_____

Location:_____

Site #:_____ Ideal Site #:_____ Date:_____

| Check In: | Check Out: | Location | ☆ ☆ ☆ ☆ ☆ |
|---|---|---|---|
| Weather: ☀ ⛅ ☁ 🌧 ⛈ | | Amenities | ☆ ☆ ☆ ☆ ☆ |
| WIFI: Good ☐ Bad ☐ None ☐ | | Cleanliness | ☆ ☆ ☆ ☆ ☆ |
| Pad Type: Dirt ☐ Concrete ☐ | | Activities | ☆ ☆ ☆ ☆ ☆ |
| Total Cost Per Night: | | Security | ☆ ☆ ☆ ☆ ☆ |

## Notes

Overall Rating: ☆ ☆ ☆ ☆ ☆    29

We went camping with: _____

_____

_____

The new people and friends that we met: _____

_____

_____

Our favorite thing to do at this campground was: ___

_____

_____

Favorite food (recipes, shops, restaurants, etc.): ___

_____

_____

We visited these cool places: _____

_____

_____

Our favorite activities that we did were: _____

_____

_____

Things we want to do and see next time: _____

_____

_____

Memorable moments or memories: _____

_____

_____

Campground:_____

Location:_____

Site #:_____ Ideal Site #:_____ Date:_____

| Check In: | Check Out: | Location | ☆ ☆ ☆ ☆ ☆ |
|---|---|---|---|
| Weather: ☀ ⛅ ☁ 🌧 ⛈ | | Amenities | ☆ ☆ ☆ ☆ ☆ |
| WIFI: Good ☐ Bad ☐ None ☐ | | Cleanliness | ☆ ☆ ☆ ☆ ☆ |
| Pad Type: Dirt ☐ Concrete ☐ | | Activities | ☆ ☆ ☆ ☆ ☆ |
| Total Cost Per Night: | | Security | ☆ ☆ ☆ ☆ ☆ |

## Notes

Overall Rating: ☆ ☆ ☆ ☆ ☆

We went camping with: _____

_____

The new people and friends that we met: _____

_____

Our favorite thing to do at this campground was: _____

_____

Favorite food (recipes, shops, restaurants, etc.): _____

_____

We visited these cool places: _____

_____

Our favorite activities that we did were: _____

_____

Things we want to do and see next time: _____

_____

Memorable moments or memories: _____

_____

_____

Campground:_____

Location:_____

Site #:_____ Ideal Site #:_____ Date:_____

| Check In: Check Out: | Location | ☆ ☆ ☆ ☆ ☆ |
|---|---|---|
| Weather: ☀ ⛅ ☁ 🌧 ⛈ | Amenities | ☆ ☆ ☆ ☆ ☆ |
| WIFI: Good ☐ Bad ☐ None ☐ | Cleanliness | ☆ ☆ ☆ ☆ ☆ |
| Pad Type: Dirt ☐ Concrete ☐ | Activities | ☆ ☆ ☆ ☆ ☆ |
| Total Cost Per Night: | Security | ☆ ☆ ☆ ☆ ☆ |

## Notes

Overall Rating: ☆ ☆ ☆ ☆ ☆     31

We went camping with: _____

_____

_____

The new people and friends that we met: _____

_____

_____

Our favorite thing to do at this campground was: _____

_____

_____

Favorite food (recipes, shops, restaurants, etc.): _____

_____

_____

We visited these cool places: _____

_____

_____

Our favorite activities that we did were: _____

_____

_____

Things we want to do and see next time: _____

_____

_____

Memorable moments or memories: _____

_____

_____

Campground:_____

Location:_____

Site #:_____ Ideal Site #:_____ Date:_____

| | | | |
|---|---|---|---|
| Check In: Check Out: | Location | ☆ ☆ ☆ ☆ ☆ |
| Weather: ☀ 🌤 ☁ 🌧 ⛈ | Amenities | ☆ ☆ ☆ ☆ ☆ |
| WIFI: Good ☐ Bad ☐ None ☐ | Cleanliness | ☆ ☆ ☆ ☆ ☆ |
| Pad Type: Dirt ☐ Concrete ☐ | Activities | ☆ ☆ ☆ ☆ ☆ |
| Total Cost Per Night: | Security | ☆ ☆ ☆ ☆ ☆ |

## Notes

Overall Rating: ☆ ☆ ☆ ☆ ☆

We went camping with: _____

_____

The new people and friends that we met: _____

_____

Our favorite thing to do at this campground was: _____

_____

Favorite food (recipes, shops, restaurants, etc.): _____

_____

We visited these cool places: _____

_____

Our favorite activities that we did were: _____

_____

Things we want to do and see next time: _____

_____

Memorable moments or memories: _____

_____

_____

Campground:_____

Location:_____

Site #:_____ Ideal Site #:_____ Date:_____

| Check In:        Check Out: | Location | ☆ ☆ ☆ ☆ ☆ |
|---|---|---|
| Weather: ☀ ⛅ ☁ 🌧 ⛈ | Amenities | ☆ ☆ ☆ ☆ ☆ |
| WIFI: Good ☐ Bad ☐ None ☐ | Cleanliness | ☆ ☆ ☆ ☆ ☆ |
| Pad Type: Dirt ☐ Concrete ☐ | Activities | ☆ ☆ ☆ ☆ ☆ |
| Total Cost Per Night: | Security | ☆ ☆ ☆ ☆ ☆ |

## Notes

Overall Rating: ☆ ☆ ☆ ☆ ☆    33

We went camping with:_____

_____

_____

The new people and friends that we met:_____

_____

_____

Our favorite thing to do at this campground was:_____

_____

_____

Favorite food (recipes, shops, restaurants, etc.):_____

_____

_____

We visited these cool places:_____

_____

_____

Our favorite activities that we did were:_____

_____

_____

Things we want to do and see next time:_____

_____

_____

Memorable moments or memories:_____

_____

_____

Campground:_____

Location:_____

Site #:_____ Ideal Site #:_____ Date:_____

| Check In:        Check Out: | Location | ☆ ☆ ☆ ☆ ☆ |
|---|---|---|
| Weather: ☀ ⛅ ☁ 🌧 ⛈ | Amenities | ☆ ☆ ☆ ☆ ☆ |
| WIFI: Good ☐ Bad ☐ None ☐ | Cleanliness | ☆ ☆ ☆ ☆ ☆ |
| Pad Type: Dirt ☐ Concrete ☐ | Activities | ☆ ☆ ☆ ☆ ☆ |
| Total Cost Per Night: | Security | ☆ ☆ ☆ ☆ ☆ |

## Notes

Overall Rating: ☆ ☆ ☆ ☆ ☆     34

We went camping with: _____

_____

The new people and friends that we met: _____

_____

Our favorite thing to do at this campground was: _____

_____

Favorite food (recipes, shops, restaurants, etc.): _____

_____

We visited these cool places: _____

_____

Our favorite activities that we did were: _____

_____

Things we want to do and see next time: _____

_____

Memorable moments or memories: _____

_____

_____

Campground:_____

Location:_____

Site #:_____ Ideal Site #:_____ Date:_____

| Check In:        Check Out: | Location | ☆ ☆ ☆ ☆ ☆ |
|---|---|---|
| Weather: ☀ ⛅ ☁ 🌧 ⛈ | Amenities | ☆ ☆ ☆ ☆ ☆ |
| WIFI: Good ☐ Bad ☐ None ☐ | Cleanliness | ☆ ☆ ☆ ☆ ☆ |
| Pad Type: Dirt ☐ Concrete ☐ | Activities | ☆ ☆ ☆ ☆ ☆ |
| Total Cost Per Night: | Security | ☆ ☆ ☆ ☆ ☆ |

## Notes

Overall Rating: ☆ ☆ ☆ ☆ ☆    35

We went camping with:_____

_____

The new people and friends that we met:_____

_____

Our favorite thing to do at this campground was:_____

_____

Favorite food (recipes, shops, restaurants, etc.):_____

_____

We visited these cool places:_____

_____

Our favorite activities that we did were:_____

_____

Things we want to do and see next time:_____

_____

Memorable moments or memories:_____

_____

_____

Campground:_____

Location:_____

Site #:_____ Ideal Site #:_____ Date:_____

| Check In:          Check Out: | Location | ☆ ☆ ☆ ☆ ☆ |
|---|---|---|
| Weather: ☀ 🌤 ☁ 🌧 ⛈ | Amenities | ☆ ☆ ☆ ☆ ☆ |
| WIFI: Good ☐ Bad ☐ None ☐ | Cleanliness | ☆ ☆ ☆ ☆ ☆ |
| Pad Type: Dirt ☐ Concrete ☐ | Activities | ☆ ☆ ☆ ☆ ☆ |
| Total Cost Per Night: | Security | ☆ ☆ ☆ ☆ ☆ |

## Notes

Overall Rating: ☆ ☆ ☆ ☆ ☆

We went camping with:_____

_____

_____

The new people and friends that we met:_____

_____

_____

Our favorite thing to do at this campground was:_____

_____

_____

Favorite food (recipes, shops, restaurants, etc.):_____

_____

_____

We visited these cool places:_____

_____

_____

Our favorite activities that we did were:_____

_____

_____

Things we want to do and see next time:_____

_____

_____

Memorable moments or memories:_____

_____

_____

Campground:

Location:

Site #:_____ Ideal Site #:_____ Date:_____

| Check In:      Check Out: | Location | ☆ ☆ ☆ ☆ ☆ |
|---|---|---|
| Weather: ☀ 🌤 ☁ 🌧 ⛈ | Amenities | ☆ ☆ ☆ ☆ ☆ |
| WIFI: Good ☐ Bad ☐ None ☐ | Cleanliness | ☆ ☆ ☆ ☆ ☆ |
| Pad Type: Dirt ☐ Concrete ☐ | Activities | ☆ ☆ ☆ ☆ ☆ |
| Total Cost Per Night: | Security | ☆ ☆ ☆ ☆ ☆ |

## Notes

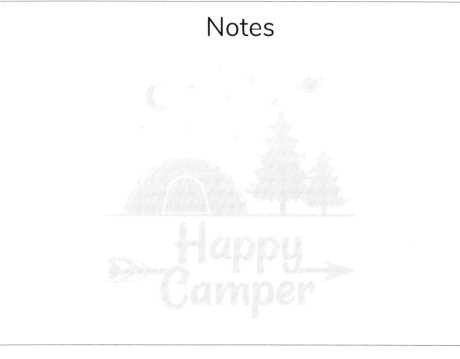

Overall Rating: ☆ ☆ ☆ ☆ ☆

We went camping with:_____

_____

_____

The new people and friends that we met:_____

_____

_____

Our favorite thing to do at this campground was:_____

_____

_____

Favorite food (recipes, shops, restaurants, etc.):_____

_____

_____

We visited these cool places:_____

_____

_____

Our favorite activities that we did were:_____

_____

_____

Things we want to do and see next time:_____

_____

_____

Memorable moments or memories:_____

_____

_____

_____

Campground:_____

Location:_____

Site #:_____ Ideal Site #:_____ Date:_____

| Check In:        Check Out: | Location | ☆ ☆ ☆ ☆ ☆ |
|---|---|---|
| Weather: ☀ ⛅ ☁ 🌧 ⛈ | Amenities | ☆ ☆ ☆ ☆ ☆ |
| WIFI: Good ☐ Bad ☐ None ☐ | Cleanliness | ☆ ☆ ☆ ☆ ☆ |
| Pad Type: Dirt ☐ Concrete ☐ | Activities | ☆ ☆ ☆ ☆ ☆ |
| Total Cost Per Night: | Security | ☆ ☆ ☆ ☆ ☆ |

## Notes

Overall Rating: ☆ ☆ ☆ ☆ ☆

We went camping with: _____

_____

_____

The new people and friends that we met: _____

_____

_____

Our favorite thing to do at this campground was: _____

_____

_____

Favorite food (recipes, shops, restaurants, etc.): _____

_____

_____

We visited these cool places: _____

_____

_____

Our favorite activities that we did were: _____

_____

_____

Things we want to do and see next time: _____

_____

_____

Memorable moments or memories: _____

_____

_____

Campground:_____

Location:_____

Site #:_____ Ideal Site #:_____ Date:_____

| Check In:          Check Out: | Location | ☆ ☆ ☆ ☆ ☆ |
|---|---|---|
| Weather: ☀ ⛅ ☁ 🌧 ⛈ | Amenities | ☆ ☆ ☆ ☆ ☆ |
| WIFI: Good ☐ Bad ☐ None ☐ | Cleanliness | ☆ ☆ ☆ ☆ ☆ |
| Pad Type: Dirt ☐ Concrete ☐ | Activities | ☆ ☆ ☆ ☆ ☆ |
| Total Cost Per Night: | Security | ☆ ☆ ☆ ☆ ☆ |

## Notes

Overall Rating: ☆ ☆ ☆ ☆ ☆   39

We went camping with: _____

_____

The new people and friends that we met: _____

_____

Our favorite thing to do at this campground was: _____

_____

Favorite food (recipes, shops, restaurants, etc.): _____

_____

We visited these cool places: _____

_____

Our favorite activities that we did were: _____

_____

Things we want to do and see next time: _____

_____

Memorable moments or memories: _____

_____

_____

Campground: _____

Location: _____

Site #: _____ Ideal Site #: _____ Date: _____

| Check In:        Check Out: | Location | ☆ ☆ ☆ ☆ ☆ |
|---|---|---|
| Weather: ☀ ⛅ ☁ 🌧 ⛈ | Amenities | ☆ ☆ ☆ ☆ ☆ |
| WIFI: Good ☐ Bad ☐ None ☐ | Cleanliness | ☆ ☆ ☆ ☆ ☆ |
| Pad Type: Dirt ☐ Concrete ☐ | Activities | ☆ ☆ ☆ ☆ ☆ |
| Total Cost Per Night: | Security | ☆ ☆ ☆ ☆ ☆ |

## Notes

Overall Rating: ☆ ☆ ☆ ☆ ☆        40

We went camping with: _____

_____

_____

The new people and friends that we met: _____

_____

_____

Our favorite thing to do at this campground was: _____

_____

_____

Favorite food (recipes, shops, restaurants, etc.): _____

_____

_____

We visited these cool places: _____

_____

_____

Our favorite activities that we did were: _____

_____

_____

Things we want to do and see next time: _____

_____

_____

Memorable moments or memories: _____

_____

_____

Campground:_____

Location:_____

Site #:_____ Ideal Site #:_____ Date:_____

| Check In:          Check Out: | Location | ☆ ☆ ☆ ☆ ☆ |
| Weather: ☀ 🌤 ☁ 🌧 ⛈ | Amenities | ☆ ☆ ☆ ☆ ☆ |
| WIFI: Good ☐ Bad ☐ None ☐ | Cleanliness | ☆ ☆ ☆ ☆ ☆ |
| Pad Type: Dirt ☐ Concrete ☐ | Activities | ☆ ☆ ☆ ☆ ☆ |
| Total Cost Per Night: | Security | ☆ ☆ ☆ ☆ ☆ |

## Notes

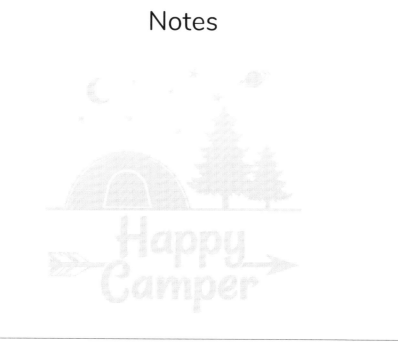

Overall Rating: ☆ ☆ ☆ ☆ ☆

We went camping with:_____

_____

_____

The new people and friends that we met:_____

_____

_____

Our favorite thing to do at this campground was:_____

_____

_____

Favorite food (recipes, shops, restaurants, etc.):_____

_____

_____

We visited these cool places:_____

_____

_____

Our favorite activities that we did were:_____

_____

_____

Things we want to do and see next time:_____

_____

_____

Memorable moments or memories:_____

_____

_____

_____

Campground:_____

Location:_____

Site #:_____ Ideal Site #:_____ Date:_____

| Check In:          Check Out: | Location | ☆ ☆ ☆ ☆ ☆ |
| --- | --- | --- |
| Weather: ☼ ⛅ ☁ 🌧 ⛈ | Amenities | ☆ ☆ ☆ ☆ ☆ |
| WIFI: Good ☐ Bad ☐ None ☐ | Cleanliness | ☆ ☆ ☆ ☆ ☆ |
| Pad Type: Dirt ☐ Concrete ☐ | Activities | ☆ ☆ ☆ ☆ ☆ |
| Total Cost Per Night: | Security | ☆ ☆ ☆ ☆ ☆ |

# Notes

Overall Rating: ☆ ☆ ☆ ☆ ☆

We went camping with: _____

_____

The new people and friends that we met: _____

_____

Our favorite thing to do at this campground was: _____

_____

Favorite food (recipes, shops, restaurants, etc.): _____

_____

We visited these cool places: _____

_____

Our favorite activities that we did were: _____

_____

_____

Things we want to do and see next time: _____

_____

_____

Memorable moments or memories: _____

_____

_____

Campground:_____

Location:_____

Site #:_____ Ideal Site #:_____ Date:_____

| Check In:        Check Out: | Location | ☆ ☆ ☆ ☆ ☆ |
|---|---|---|
| Weather: ☀ ⛅ ☁ 🌧 ⛈ | Amenities | ☆ ☆ ☆ ☆ ☆ |
| WIFI: Good ☐ Bad ☐ None ☐ | Cleanliness | ☆ ☆ ☆ ☆ ☆ |
| Pad Type: Dirt ☐ Concrete ☐ | Activities | ☆ ☆ ☆ ☆ ☆ |
| Total Cost Per Night: | Security | ☆ ☆ ☆ ☆ ☆ |

## Notes

Overall Rating: ☆ ☆ ☆ ☆ ☆

We went camping with: _____

_____

_____

The new people and friends that we met: _____

_____

_____

Our favorite thing to do at this campground was: _____

_____

_____

Favorite food (recipes, shops, restaurants, etc.): _____

_____

_____

We visited these cool places: _____

_____

_____

Our favorite activities that we did were: _____

_____

_____

Things we want to do and see next time: _____

_____

_____

Memorable moments or memories: _____

_____

_____

Campground:_____

Location:_____

Site #:_____ Ideal Site #:_____ Date:_____

| Check In:        Check Out: | Location | ☆ ☆ ☆ ☆ ☆ |
| Weather: ☀ ⛅ ☁ 🌧 ⛈ | Amenities | ☆ ☆ ☆ ☆ ☆ |
| WIFI: Good ☐ Bad ☐ None ☐ | Cleanliness | ☆ ☆ ☆ ☆ ☆ |
| Pad Type: Dirt ☐ Concrete ☐ | Activities | ☆ ☆ ☆ ☆ ☆ |
| Total Cost Per Night: | Security | ☆ ☆ ☆ ☆ ☆ |

## Notes

Overall Rating: ☆ ☆ ☆ ☆ ☆     44

We went camping with: _____

_____

The new people and friends that we met: _____

_____

Our favorite thing to do at this campground was: _____

_____

Favorite food (recipes, shops, restaurants, etc.): _____

_____

We visited these cool places: _____

_____

Our favorite activities that we did were: _____

_____

Things we want to do and see next time: _____

_____

Memorable moments or memories: _____

_____

_____

Campground:_____

Location:_____

Site #:_____ Ideal Site #:_____ Date:_____

| Check In:     Check Out: | Location | ☆ ☆ ☆ ☆ ☆ |
|---|---|---|
| Weather: ☀ ⛅ ☁ 🌧 ⛈ | Amenities | ☆ ☆ ☆ ☆ ☆ |
| WIFI: Good ☐ Bad ☐ None ☐ | Cleanliness | ☆ ☆ ☆ ☆ ☆ |
| Pad Type: Dirt ☐ Concrete ☐ | Activities | ☆ ☆ ☆ ☆ ☆ |
| Total Cost Per Night: | Security | ☆ ☆ ☆ ☆ ☆ |

## Notes

Overall Rating: ☆ ☆ ☆ ☆ ☆       45

We went camping with:_____

_____

The new people and friends that we met:_____

_____

Our favorite thing to do at this campground was:_____

_____

Favorite food (recipes, shops, restaurants, etc.):_____

_____

We visited these cool places:_____

_____

Our favorite activities that we did were:_____

_____

Things we want to do and see next time:_____

_____

Memorable moments or memories:_____

_____

_____

Campground:_____

Location:_____

Site #:_____ Ideal Site #:_____ Date:_____

| Check In:     Check Out: | Location | ☆ ☆ ☆ ☆ ☆ |
|---|---|---|
| Weather: ☀ ⛅ ☁ 🌧 ⛈ | Amenities | ☆ ☆ ☆ ☆ ☆ |
| WIFI: Good ☐ Bad ☐ None ☐ | Cleanliness | ☆ ☆ ☆ ☆ ☆ |
| Pad Type: Dirt ☐ Concrete ☐ | Activities | ☆ ☆ ☆ ☆ ☆ |
| Total Cost Per Night: | Security | ☆ ☆ ☆ ☆ ☆ |

## Notes

Overall Rating: ☆ ☆ ☆ ☆ ☆    46

We went camping with: _____

_____

The new people and friends that we met: _____

_____

Our favorite thing to do at this campground was: _____

_____

Favorite food (recipes, shops, restaurants, etc.): _____

_____

We visited these cool places: _____

_____

Our favorite activities that we did were: _____

_____

Things we want to do and see next time: _____

_____

Memorable moments or memories: _____

_____

_____

Campground:_____

Location:_____

Site #:_____ Ideal Site #:_____ Date:_____

| Check In:          Check Out: | Location | ☆ ☆ ☆ ☆ ☆ |
| --- | --- | --- |
| Weather: ☼ ⛅ ☁ 🌧 ⛈ | Amenities | ☆ ☆ ☆ ☆ ☆ |
| WIFI: Good ☐ Bad ☐ None ☐ | Cleanliness | ☆ ☆ ☆ ☆ ☆ |
| Pad Type: Dirt ☐ Concrete ☐ | Activities | ☆ ☆ ☆ ☆ ☆ |
| Total Cost Per Night: | Security | ☆ ☆ ☆ ☆ ☆ |

## Notes

Overall Rating: ☆ ☆ ☆ ☆ ☆       47

We went camping with: _____

_____

The new people and friends that we met: _____

_____

Our favorite thing to do at this campground was: _____

_____

Favorite food (recipes, shops, restaurants, etc.): _____

_____

We visited these cool places: _____

_____

Our favorite activities that we did were: _____

_____

Things we want to do and see next time: _____

_____

Memorable moments or memories: _____

_____

_____

Campground:_____

Location:_____

Site #:_____ Ideal Site #:_____ Date:_____

| Check In:          Check Out: | Location | ☆ ☆ ☆ ☆ ☆ |
|---|---|---|
| Weather: ☀ ⛅ ☁ 🌧 ⛈ | Amenities | ☆ ☆ ☆ ☆ ☆ |
| WIFI: Good ☐ Bad ☐ None ☐ | Cleanliness | ☆ ☆ ☆ ☆ ☆ |
| Pad Type: Dirt ☐ Concrete ☐ | Activities | ☆ ☆ ☆ ☆ ☆ |
| Total Cost Per Night: | Security | ☆ ☆ ☆ ☆ ☆ |

## Notes

Overall Rating: ☆ ☆ ☆ ☆ ☆   48

We went camping with: _____

_____

_____

The new people and friends that we met: _____

_____

_____

Our favorite thing to do at this campground was: _____

_____

_____

Favorite food (recipes, shops, restaurants, etc.): _____

_____

_____

We visited these cool places: _____

_____

_____

Our favorite activities that we did were: _____

_____

_____

Things we want to do and see next time: _____

_____

_____

Memorable moments or memories: _____

_____

_____

Campground:_____

Location:_____

Site #:_____ Ideal Site #:_____ Date:_____

| Check In:          Check Out: | Location | ☆ ☆ ☆ ☆ ☆ |
|---|---|---|
| Weather: ☀ ⛅ ☁ 🌧 ⛈ | Amenities | ☆ ☆ ☆ ☆ ☆ |
| WIFI: Good ☐ Bad ☐ None ☐ | Cleanliness | ☆ ☆ ☆ ☆ ☆ |
| Pad Type: Dirt ☐ Concrete ☐ | Activities | ☆ ☆ ☆ ☆ ☆ |
| Total Cost Per Night: | Security | ☆ ☆ ☆ ☆ ☆ |

## Notes

Overall Rating: ☆ ☆ ☆ ☆ ☆     49

We went camping with:_____

_____

The new people and friends that we met:_____

_____

Our favorite thing to do at this campground was:_____

_____

Favorite food (recipes, shops, restaurants, etc.):_____

_____

We visited these cool places:_____

_____

Our favorite activities that we did were:_____

_____

Things we want to do and see next time:_____

_____

Memorable moments or memories:_____

_____

_____

Campground:_____

Location:_____

Site #:_____ Ideal Site #:_____ Date:_____

| Check In:          Check Out: | Location | ☆ ☆ ☆ ☆ ☆ |
| --- | --- | --- |
| Weather: ☀ ⛅ ☁ 🌧 ⛈ | Amenities | ☆ ☆ ☆ ☆ ☆ |
| WIFI: Good ☐ Bad ☐ None ☐ | Cleanliness | ☆ ☆ ☆ ☆ ☆ |
| Pad Type: Dirt ☐ Concrete ☐ | Activities | ☆ ☆ ☆ ☆ ☆ |
| Total Cost Per Night: | Security | ☆ ☆ ☆ ☆ ☆ |

## Notes

Overall Rating: ☆ ☆ ☆ ☆ ☆  50

We went camping with: _____

_____

The new people and friends that we met: _____

_____

Our favorite thing to do at this campground was: _____

_____

Favorite food (recipes, shops, restaurants, etc.): _____

_____

We visited these cool places: _____

_____

Our favorite activities that we did were: _____

_____

Things we want to do and see next time: _____

_____

Memorable moments or memories: _____

_____

_____

Manufactured by Amazon.ca
Bolton, ON

18673660R00059